SAMMY
DOG DETECTIVE

SAMMY
DOG DETECTIVE

BY
Colleen Stanley Bare

SCHOLASTIC INC.
New York Toronto London Auckland Sydney
Mexico City New Delhi Hong Kong

To Andy

ACKNOWLEDGMENTS

The author wishes to thank police officer Andy Schlenker for his invaluable assistance with this project, and also to acknowledge the helpful support of his wife, Anita, and children, Nick and Gene. The cooperation of the Modesto, California, City Police Department K-9 Unit under the supervision of Sgt. Gene Balentine is also greatly appreciated.

ISBN 0-439-15982-2

12 11 10 9 8 7 6 5 4

0 1 2 3 4 5/0

Printed in the U.S.A.

24

First Scholastic printing, February 2000

Designed by Charlotte Staub

Sammy is like most pet dogs.
He is lovable, huggable, friendly,
and tries to steal kisses.

He is also different from most pet dogs,
because Sammy is a dog detective.
He works for a police department
eight hours a day,
five days a week.

Sammy is the canine part of a K-9 team.
The other half is a police officer named Andy.
The two work together to protect people
and property. They also live together,
because Sammy is Andy's family dog.

Both of Sammy's parents were working
police dogs. His K-9 mother was a German
Shepherd, the breed most often used in police
work. His K-9 father was a Belgian Malinois,
known for its intelligence and speed.
Sammy has the best traits of both.
He is smart, strong, fast,
loyal, and brave.

STAY AWAY
POLICE DOG

The team of Andy and Sammy does many jobs.
When Andy commands, the dog searches areas,
buildings, and cars. Just the sight of big,
barking Sammy scares most criminals.
They usually put up their hands and shout,
"Don't let him bite me. I give up!"
Sammy also helps Andy find
missing persons and
control crowds.

How did Sammy learn to be a police dog?
He couldn't read about it in a book,

HOW TO BE
A GOOD
POLICE
DOG

or on a computer.

Instead, Sammy went to K-9
school, starting at age one year.
He trained almost every day.
At eighteen months, he was the
youngest dog ever to pass
the K-9 tests in his
police department.

Sammy's first training was in **obedience**.
He was taught to heel, or to go to Andy's
left side — and to come, stay, sit,
lie down, and bark.
He also learned hand signals for each.
They are used when Sammy is too far away
to hear or if quiet is needed.

HEEL

SIT

LIE DOWN

BARK

Next came lessons in agility, search, and attack.
These are skills that he often needs at work.
Agility training involves jumping and
climbing, which Sammy
really enjoys.
He climbs ladders and over barrels and walls.
He jumps hurdles and through open windows.
He walks on narrow planks above the ground
and crawls through tunnels.

Search training uses Sammy's super sense
of smell. When Andy says "track," the dog puts
his nose to the ground and starts sniffing.
To locate hidden objects out-of-doors, such as a
gun or knife, he hunts for any articles that smell
different to him. When he finds one, he barks.
Not only does he sniff out weapons, he also may
bark at a comb, shoe, bottle cap, piece of paper,
anything unusual in that setting.

Sometimes Sammy is ordered to find a person
hiding inside one of several large wooden
boxes. Sammy sniffs each box until he
detects the human. Then he barks
until Andy summons him.

When Andy and Sammy hunt for someone
inside a building, Andy gives Sammy
the command "search." The dog runs
through the building, sniffing, until
he discovers the suspect. Sammy
barks until Andy calls him back.
The dog has been trained to "bark instead of
bite" and never to bite unless Andy tells him
to do so. Although Sammy has assisted in at
least one hundred arrests, he has only had
to bite twice. Each time the "bad guy"
was running away. One was a burglar.
The other had hit a policeman.

Attack training is difficult for some dogs, but not
for brave Sammy. When a trainer wearing a
padded sleeve waves a club at Sammy,
Andy says "get him!" Sammy leaps at
the trainer's protected arm, grabs it
with his teeth, and holds on. He
only lets go when Andy says
"out," meaning "let go."
Sammy's ability to attack on command could
save Andy's life or his own some day.

Fireworks are used to teach Sammy to ignore
loud sounds such as gunfire. He also learns
to enter buildings filled with smoke,
created by using smoke bombs.

These lessons are repeated over and over.
When Sammy makes a mistake, patient
Andy never hits him. He just says
"no!" and shows disapproval.
He rewards Sammy's good behavior by saying
"good boy" — and with a hug, a pat,
and often a treat.

Sammy trains for several hours each week
and for a full day once a month.
He gets extra practice by entering many police
K-9 contests. He competes with up to
sixty dogs in obedience, agility,
search, and attack.

Sammy has won trophies in every K-9 trial he
has ever entered. He is ranked as "Number
One" police dog in the Western States
Police Canine Association.

Sammy leads two lives. He is a tough dog detective, working for the police. And he is a beloved pet, living at home with his family. He does almost everything that the family does. At night, he sleeps on Andy's or the children's beds, causing crowding.

In the morning, Sammy brings in the sometimes slobbery newspaper.

He has
frequent
baths,

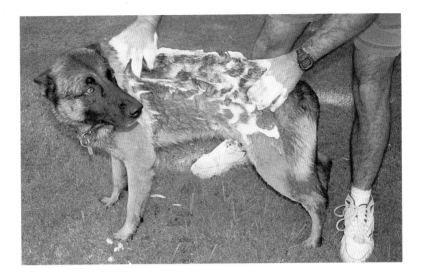

and gets
his teeth
brushed.

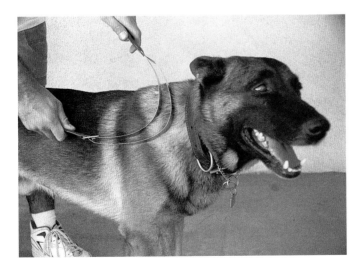

His coat is
groomed with
a special
tool.

Sammy plays ball and swims
with the children.

Sammy shares in family
picnics, vacations, and celebrations.
At Christmas, he has his own presents.
His favorite is a rawhide bone.

23

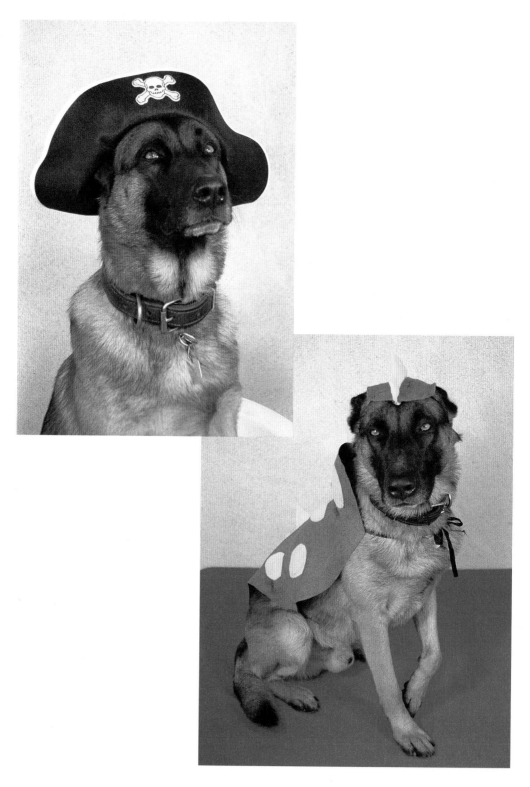

Sammy goes trick-or-treating on Halloween.
The children put hats on him.
One year he was a dinosaur.

Another year he was a pirate.

Children love Sammy, and Sammy
loves children.

Andy and Sammy give K-9 programs at schools.
The students laugh when Sammy jumps
in and out of a police car window.

Everyone wants to pat Sammy.

He reaches for kisses.

Sammy loves being a police dog.
On his days off, when he can't go to work,
he gets bored and sometimes howls.

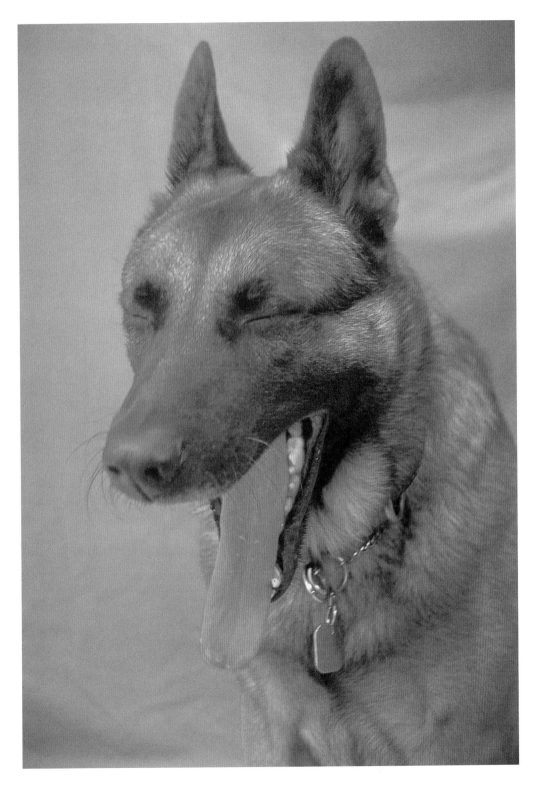

Sammy and Andy are close friends.
They are a team, working together to make
their world a safer place.

INDEX

DATE DUE